# Bruiser
# A True Story About a Special Cat

WRITTEN BY BARBARA ANN GAREIS

ILLUSTRATED BY SKYLER BAJEK

# DEDICATION

For Bruiser's friends and fans who have supported him since his rescue,
we could not have provided the treatment and care he deserves without your help.
Thank you from the bottom of our hearts.

And a special thank you to all those associated with Bordentown City Cats, the entire staff of Columbus Central Veterinary Hospital, editor Elizabeth Buege, and friend Jill Grow with Jill Lynn Photography. You have all gone above and beyond in showing so much love to Bruiser and supporting this project. We cannot thank you enough.

A special cat wandered all around town.
He was quite dirty. His white spots looked brown.

The other cats teased him. They wanted to fight.
A lady tried to stop them, but one cat liked to bite.

All the cats ran except the special cat.
He stayed where he was, and that's where he sat.

The lady called Animal Control. Officer George arrived fast. "All the other cats ran," she said. "He is the last."

"He bit me," she said as she pointed at Bruiser.
But it wasn't this cat. The other cats had confused her.

In his truck, George held Bruiser so he wouldn't fall.
Bruiser yawned, and George saw almost no teeth at all.

"This cat didn't bite her. I doubt he'd hurt a mouse!
She must be mistaken. I'm taking this cat to my house."

When Bruiser met George's wife, he started to purr.
He lay in her lap while she stroked his thick fur.

"You're special," she told him. "You're missing your ears.
You have a bad eye, and I see a few tears."

"Were you lost and alone? Scared of the dark?
Did giant dogs chase you? Did they snarl and bark?"

He hopped from her lap and hobbled away.
She followed him, thinking he might want to play.

"What's wrong with your leg? Is that limping I see?
Did somebody hurt you? Did you fall from a tree?

He lay in the corner with his chin on the floor.
She found a few toys and told George they'd need more.

"You've been scared and alone for so very long.
But you're a special cat, and you are quite strong."

"I'll give you a home. You can sleep in my bed.
I'll hug you and kiss you, and you will be fed."

"You are so special. You're a gift from above.
You're my best buddy—a new friend to love."

"You will no longer be lonely or misunderstood.
You will be loved and cared for, as all animals should."

Later that day, the family went to the store.
They bought food, treats, and toys, and quite a bit more.

When they returned home, Bruiser was pleased.
Now the special cat would no longer be teased.

Bruiser finally had a home and a safe place to sleep.
The special cat found love and a family to keep.

Read more about Bruiser at www.bruisercat.com
and follow him on Facebook at
www.facebook.com/bruiserlovesyou.

# Bruiser and His Family

Barbara Gareis

George Gareis

## ABOUT THE AUTHOR

Barbara Ann Gareis is an author, blogger, and speaker. She has a business degree and lives in NJ with her husband George who is an animal control officer and animal cruelty investigator. They have two grown kids, two dogs, and several cats.

## ABOUT THE ILLUSTRATOR

Skyler Bajek is a high school art student who lives with her family in NJ. She is in her second year of graphic arts at MCTS and plans on studying graphic arts and graphic communications in college. She also enjoys playing field hockey.

Made in the USA
Coppell, TX
16 September 2020